The Story of the Easter Rising, 1916

John Dorney

Published by Green Lamp Editions

Published by Green Lamp Editions
© John Dorney 2010
Typeset by cbdigitize.com
Createspace Edition
ISBN: 9781907694042

Contents

Introduction

The Easter Rising can be summed in just a few sentences. On 24 April 1916, approximately 1,200 armed Irish Republican separatists of the Irish Volunteers occupied public buildings in Dublin city centre and proclaimed an Irish Republic, independent of Britain. They occupied them for just under a week, in which the British deployed up to 16,000 troops, artillery and a naval gunboat to the city to dislodge them, before they surrendered. The rebellion's principal leaders were executed and the remainder imprisoned.

The fighting cost the lives of around 500 people, of whom roughly half were civilians.[1] If that had been the end of the matter, then perhaps that summary would suffice. However, the Easter Rising turned out to be a beginning rather than an end. WB Yeats wrote of it, "a terrible beauty is born". The "beauty", was the revival of militant, physical force Irish nationalism, which had lain dormant for over fifty years.

Within two years of the rebellion, in 1918, Republican separatists had won a general election in Ireland and proclaimed an Irish Republic – this time with an electoral mandate. By the sixth anniversary of the Rising in 1924, Ireland was partitioned into two states, one of which, the Irish Free State, traced its origins to the Proclamation of the Republic in 1916. The other, Northern Ireland, was bitterly hostile to Rising and its legacy.

Nor was that all. Guerrilla warfare and political violence from 1919–23, in large part inspired by the "blood sacrifice" of 1916, had claimed up to 4,000 more lives.[2] The Irish Republican Army, descendant of the Irish Volunteers, had waged a guerrilla campaign against British rule in defence of the Republic. And when the Anglo-Irish treaty of 1921 replaced that Republic with a Free State, they had fought that too. In short, the Rising had complex, bloody and long-term results.

For this reason, even now, almost a century later, the legacy of the events of April 1916 are still bitterly debated. For Irish republicans it is the touchstone of their political faith. It is the origin of their claim to complete Irish independence and the justification of their right to take up arms in pursuit of this. For the Irish state, now the Republic of Ireland, the Rising has sometimes been bombastically commemorated and sometimes bundled nervously into a dark corner along with other parts of the state's dark and violent origins. For those loyal to the Union with Britain, now principally concentrated in Northern Ireland, the Rising was always a treacherous stab in the back of Britain and of the Irishmen serving her in the First World War.

However, even in nationalist Ireland, a strain of thought since the 1970s, known as "revisionist" in Irish historical circles, has portrayed the Rising as an undemocratic act by an unrepresentative minority. For them it founded a militarist "cult of violence" around Irish republican politics which has haunted both Irish states up to the present. It will be obvious, therefore, that no account of Easter 1916 can hope to be completely neutral and this one will contain the views and biases of the author. Nevertheless, this piece will not try to argue for the acceptance of any one of the competing interpretations of the Rising. It will hope merely to tell its story.

Part I: Ireland in 1916

In 1916, Ireland was a part of the United Kingdom of Great Britain and Ireland, in just the same manner as England, Scotland or Wales. It had been since the Irish Parliament was abolished in 1801. But it was a very unusual part. It had elections, which were increasingly democratic as the franchise was extended. It sent 103 MPs to the Westminster Parliament, to sit among 566 Members from the rest of UK. Yet in no sense did Ireland's elected representatives run the country. Ireland at the dawn of the twentieth century was ruled by a British, principally English, administration, based in Dublin. Power in Ireland was held by three men, only one of them elected, and none of them Irish.

The first was the Lord Lieutenant, the King's representative in Ireland, who was usually an English aristocrat and who was based in the Vice-Regal Lodge in Dublin's Phoenix Park. His position was increasingly symbolic, but like the King himself, he had the right to hold up laws and to advise the Executive branch of government. In 1916, this position was held by Ivor Churchill, Baron of Wimborne.

Executive power lay in the hands of the Chief Secretary for Ireland, who was an MP appointed by the incumbent government in Britain. The Chief Secretary from 1908 to 1916 was Augustine Birrell. He was a liberal, both in the sense of belonging to the Liberal Party and in that he believed his role was to prepare Ireland for self-government and to peacefully redress long-standing Irish grievances.

The third prong of this trident was the Under Secretary for Ireland. This, unlike the Chief Secretary, was a permanent position, based in Dublin Castle – the centre of English rule in Ireland for over 700 years – and responsible for day to day running of the country. It was held in 1916 by Mathew Nathan.

The personnel in the higher levels of the Irish administration, were, moreover, all British. A French observer living in Dublin thought British regime in Ireland was underlain by deep-rooted prejudice, "a gentle, quiet, well meaning, established, unconscious, inborn contempt".[3]

Thus Ireland was neither entirely a colony – since it had its own elected representatives – nor entirely democratic, since power lay with London and with their appointees in Dublin. Moreover, the large majority of Irish MPs – in 1910, 84 out of 103 – were nationalists of one form or another seeking self-government for Ireland.[4] And Irish nationalism, even when expressed in constitutional terms, was not loyal to the status quo.

This was the fundamental contradiction of British rule in Ireland by the early 20th century and the one that left it vulnerable to revolt. The United Kingdom was increasingly democratic as voting rights were extended to the working classes. The superiority of the elected House of Commons over the House of Lords was asserted by Liberal governments in 1900–1910. It was dependent on a broadly based agreement that those in power were there by the will of the majority of the governed. In Ireland, this consensus just did not exist. Why not?

Looking Back

To answer this needs a step backwards into history. Ireland, had in various stages, been conquered and colonized by England between the 12th and 16th centuries. Until the Act of Union of 1801 put an end to Irish self-government, power in the country, political, economic and social, was held by a small, Protestant landed elite – largely of English origin. Catholics, the large majority of the population, were excluded from land-owning and political power. Under the Act of Union in 1801, the Kingdom of Ireland was incorporated into the United Kingdom. The 19th century, Catholic grievances were slowly redressed by the British state. First the came Catholic Emancipation in 1829 which allowed Catholics to hold public office. Then in the 1870s–1890s, following militant and sometimes violent agitation by the nationalist Land League, tenant farmers were subsidized to buy their holdings from their landlords, undermining the economic power of the still largely Protestant, landed gentry. The Protestant Church of Ireland was disestablished in 1869 meaning that it was no longer supported by a compulsory tax.

Finally, with the extension of right to vote, Catholics became represented in a mass-based Party – the Irish Parliamentary Party, often called simply "the Irish Party" – which rapidly became the largest in the country. Protestants, especially in Ulster, organized themselves from the 1880s as "Unionists" – i.e. defenders of the Union and the British connection. In 1895, the British extended the powers of local government in Ireland, effectively devolving local power to Nationalist and Catholic representatives where they were a majority.[5]

This story had an enormous bearing in the 1916 Rising and all that came after. Firstly, Irish Catholics had never been entirely integrated into the English or British states in Ireland. Their historical memory of the state was of disaffection and sometimes violent repression. The Royal Irish Constabulary, alone among the police forces of the United Kingdom, was armed, with carbines and revolvers, and was taught military drill.[6]

Moreover, unlike other police forces in the United Kingdom, it was responsible directly to the Irish Executive – that is, the Chief Secretary for Ireland – and not, as in England, to local elected representatives.[7] Many Irish rural communities had experienced violent confrontation with the forces of law and order as they were built up during the 19th century. Irish Catholic nationalism, was therefore, at best, "semi-loyal" to the United Kingdom.[8] It accepted the status quo sometimes, but with qualifications. During the Boer War (1899–1901), Irish nationalists had often supported the Boers, or at least shown them sympathy. Some Irishmen in South Africa itself had even fought on their side against the British Empire.[9]

Secondly, while power in Ireland was held by English appointees – a grievance in and of itself – senior positions in the civil and public service in 1916 were still predominantly held by Irish Protestants. Catholics were making progress redressing this balance, but slowly.[10] Todd Andrews, a youthful rebel in 1916, later recalled, "we Catholics varied socially among ourselves, but we all had a common bond, whatever our economic condition, of being second class citizens".[11] Moreover, religious conflict, without nationalist or political elements was still present in Irish society. In Dublin, for example, the Catholic Church and Protestant evangelical societies competed fiercely for converts in the inner-city slums.[12]

Thirdly, and perhaps most importantly, the story of the Catholics as the indigenous Irish majority, in the past unjustly dispossessed of their land and independence by "England", was the story Irish Catholics told about themselves. The advent of cheap or free Catholic education in the late 19th century reinforced this. The Christian Brothers, in particular, educated a generation of future rebels including Patrick Pearse, Cathal Brugha and many others, with a strongly nationalist and Catholic version of Irish history. One Volunteer fighter during the Easter Rising found himself, "thinking of my school days, the lectures the Christian Brothers had gave us... about the Mass Rock and the Famine and blessed Oliver Plunkett and of Emmet and Tone, McCracken and Sheares.[13]

This is not to say that Irish nationalism and Irish Catholicism were interchangeable phrases. They were not. The goal of Irish nationalism, and particularly the more virulent brand known as Irish Republicanism, was an independent Ireland, "for all Irishmen, irrespective of class or creed". Nationalist leaders had often been Protestant – from Wolfe Tone, the republican revolutionary executed for landing with a French expeditionary force in 1798, to Charles Stewart Parnell, who had led the Land League and the Irish Party in the 1870s and 1880s. Closer to 1916, two of the most senior and active figures in the Irish Republican Brotherhood, Ernest Blythe and Bulmer Hobson, were both Ulster Protestants.

Nevertheless, Irish nationalism was an intensely Catholic phenomenon. The rebels of 1916 blessed the flag of the Irish Republic with holy water before going into battle and said the Rosary before

7

and during the fighting. On the first day of the rebellion, Joseph Plunkett, one of the Rising's leaders, paid a visit to the Catholic Bishop's Palace in Drumcondra to inform the Archbishop of Dublin of the impending insurrection. A few weeks before, his father, a Papal Count, had visited the Pope himself, to tell him of his son's plans.[14] The communal solidarity and political identity of Irish Catholics therefore, gave Irish nationalism a base of support that was to prove powerful and enduring.

Part II: The Home Rule Crisis

So British rule in Ireland, if it was to be democratic, was founded on an inherent contradiction. It could govern based on the consent of a minority – Irish Protestants. It could govern by force without reference to either Irish political community. But it could not govern with the consent of the majority – Irish Catholics. The solution was to let the majority govern themselves. Irish self-government became known as "Home Rule".

This idea did not come easily to many in Westminster at the height of the British Empire. It took a formidable popular mobilization in the Irish Party and the Land League to get it on the agenda. It also took a strategic alliance between the Irish Party and the Liberals in Britain in the Westminster Parliament. Home Rule Bills, which would have given Ireland a limited autonomy – no control over customs, foreign policy or defence – were drafted in 1886, 1895 and 1912.

Each time they were drafted however, they were stalled by the opposition of powerful groups on either side of the Irish sea. The Irish Unionists, almost exclusively Protestant and concentrated in north-east Ulster, objected to Home Rule on two grounds. The first was openly sectarian: they would not live under Catholic government. "Home Rule is Rome Rule", their slogan went.[15] The second was economic. Only the north-east had had an industrial revolution. Belfast's factories and shipyards needed access to British and Imperial markets. Southern agriculture needed protection against them. Northern industrialists therefore threw their weight behind Unionism.[16]

The Unionists were aided by the British Conservative Party with whom they shared an ideology of Imperial unity, and with whom they had a close Parliamentary alliance.[17] The first two Home Rule Bills were stalled by the Conservative-dominated House of Lords. By the time of the Third in 1912, the Liberal government had taken on and defeated the upper house in battle over their budget of 1910, which the Lords had not wanted to approve. The elected government now had the right to make law whatever Bills it passed and Home Rule could not be stopped in Westminster.

For this reason, the Unionist opposition shifted to direct action. Mass meetings were organized. The "Ulster Covenant" of 1912 saw almost 500,000 unionist men and women sign an oath to resist Home Rule. In November 1913, a Unionist militia, the Ulster Volunteer Force was formed. It was armed surreptitiously over the following year. In response, nationalists formed their own paramilitary force, the Irish Volunteers with the intention, not of fighting the Ulster Volunteers, but of applying equal pressure to guarantee the passage of Home Rule. Eoin MacNeill, the founder of the Volunteers, was a Gaelic League scholar and academic. He wrote that the Volunteers would "show the Tories that the alternative to Home Rule was a policy of repression and coercion beyond any they had experience of" and "show the Ulster minority that nationalist Ireland could not be treated with contempt".[18]

Elements of the British Army based in the Curragh refused to act against the Unionists in March 1914, despite their widespread and illegal importation of arms. On the other hand, when the Irish

Volunteers landed rifles at Howth in July 1914, the British troops, after a failed attempt to seize the guns, fired on a taunting nationalist crowd at Bachelor's Walk in Dublin, killing four and wounding 37.[19]

Meanwhile, the implementation of Home Rule stalled. John Redmond, the leader of the Irish Party, took part in three-way talks with the British Government and Unionist leader Carson. For the first time the partition of Ireland into north and south was mooted. The crisis, which looked increasingly menacing, involving as it did two large and armed private militias, was suddenly eclipsed however, by a greater one. In August 1914, war broke out in Europe and Britain declared war on Germany. John Redmond and William Carson, both keen to show their loyalty, agreed to postpone a final settlement until after the war, and called on their followers to enlist in the British Armed forces. Over 200,000 Irishmen would go on to serve in the First World War and almost 30,000 would die in it.[20] This convergence of circumstances – the frustration of constitutional nationalist demands by Unionist defiance, the formation of armed paramilitary groupings, the apparent bias of the British response to them, and the opportunity and military aid offered by Britain's entry into a major European war – was a combustible cocktail. Taken together they would give the opportunity to the most radical elements of Irish nationalism for armed rebellion.

Part III: Radical Separatism

The Easter Rising, it is important to remember, was not carried out by a Catholic nationalist mass movement, nor by frustrated Home Rulers, nor by a sectarian opposition to the Ulster Volunteers. The Rising was, first of all, the product of a small secretive conspiracy – to the extent that most of the Irish population had no idea of its existence until it was underway and no clear idea of its composition or motivation until well after it was over. To understand why and how the rebellion came about, it is necessary to look at a smaller but altogether more committed world – that of radical Irish separatism.

The Proclamation of the Irish Republic, published on the first day of the rebellion, declared that, "In every generation the Irish people have asserted their right to national freedom and sovereignty: six times during the past three hundred years they have asserted it in arms".[21] To take the last three, insurrections aimed at the toppling of British rule in Ireland had been attempted in 1803, 1848 and 1867. In the first two instances, liberal Protestants – Robert Emmet and the Young Ireland movement respectively, inspired by continental republicanism – had taken up arms but been suppressed after relatively minor skirmishes. In the second half of the 19th century, the Irish Republican Brotherhood (IRB) or Fenians, had built up a substantial underground organization, with up to 40,000 members, mostly among the rural, Catholic working class.[22] They were dedicated to open insurrection to topple British rule. In 1867, the IRB tried to launch a rebellion but it collapsed through poor organization and Government infiltration. In the aftermath, the Fenians carried out a number of dynamite attacks in Britain itself, aimed at freeing their prisoners there.

In 1879, the leaders of "The Organization", as its members called it decided on a "New Departure", eschewing, for now, physical force in favour of adopting the land question and building a broad nationalist movement.[23] Armed rebellion would not be pursued again until it had mass backing from the people. The Fenians, therefore, were a significant but mostly unseen presence in the land agitation from the 1870s onwards and in the rise of the Irish Party,[24] though they afterwards grew disillusioned with the constitutional movement. So a significant tradition of armed, conspiratorial nationalism existed in early twentieth century Ireland. Two more things should be stated about "Fenianism". First, it had always had a slightly anti-clerical flavour. The Catholic Church had denounced in the 19th century, as a "lawless" and "Godless" secret society. The Fenians, in response, though overwhelmingly Catholic in origin, had always asserted their right to separate politics and religion. Second, the IRB had always had a powerful presence in America, through its sister organization, Clan na Gael. The Clan were a valuable source of funds, arms and as a place of refuge if Ireland became too uncomfortable.

The IRB, which had lapsed into something of a debating club in the early years of the 20th century, was revived as a militant force by the efforts of a small number of energetic activists. Starting from Belfast, Dennis McCullough (a Belfast Catholic) and Bulmer Hobson (a county Down Quaker) had reinvigorated The Organization – sending activists across the country to organize cells, or "circles" in IRB terminology. By 1916, the IRB had 1,300 members in Ireland.[25] It was not a guerrilla army, rather something resembling a secret revolutionary vanguard. Nevertheless, its circles did have guns and sometimes used them. In Clare and Galway for example, local IRB men fired shots in local land agitation in the years before the Rising.[26]

From 1909, two IRB leaders in particular, Tom Clarke and Sean McDermott, had pressed for some kind of armed uprising.[27] The IRB was instrumental in the founding of the Irish Volunteers, which provided an open and popular armed organization which could be directed to separatist ends. Most of the initial leadership were IRB men.[28] However, the existence of the IRB alone, with its uncomplicated doctrine of complete Irish independence by any means necessary, cannot explain the Rising. They operated within a wider pool of radical Irish nationalism.

Irish society changed rapidly and at times painfully in the second half of the 19th century, after the terrible famine of the 1840s, which killed up to a million people. Marriages took place much later in life, so that land did not have to sub-divided and holdings could be preserved in economic sizes. Literacy shot up in the following generations, as did social mobility. The extensive construction of railways and the beginnings of mass consumer culture also opened Irish Catholic life up to a much broader, though primarily British, frame of references.

While some of these reactions to the cataclysm of the 1840s would appear positive, a section of Irish people viewed their result – an English-speaking, British-influenced mass culture – as the slow murder of Irish identity. Patrick Pearse thought that if the language was allowed to die by his generation, "they would go down to their graves with the knowledge that their children and their children's children cursed their memory".[29] In the 1851 census, 23% of the Irish population used Irish as their first language. By 1901 it was only 14%.[30] The fear of the permanent loss of what made Ireland unique led to the formation of two important organizations. First came the Gaelic League, dedicated to the revival of the Irish language, and second the Gaelic Athletic Association (GAA), which promoted indigenous Irish games – hurling and Gaelic football – over "English" ones such as soccer, rugby and cricket.

Two points should be made about the phenomenon of "cultural nationalism". The first is that it was as much a re-invention as a revival. The Gaelic League was founded by Douglas Hyde and Eoin MacNeill (future founder of the Volunteer movement) in 1893 in Dublin, where the English language had been predominant since at least the mid 18th century.[31] Many of its early adherents – notably Douglas Hyde and Maud Gonne – were "Anglo-Irish" (of the Protestant upper class), whose ancestors had most likely never spoken the language in the first place. Patrick Pearse, the principal Gaelic League ideologue of the Easter Rising, had an English father. All of them learned Irish as adults. In the remaining Irish speaking areas or *Gaeltachtaí*, the language continued to decline in spite of the League's efforts. However, the idea of a "Gaelic revival" provided the basis to imagine a new Ireland formed on the basis of its "true" nature prior to English conquest.

Into this bottle could be poured almost anything nationalist revolutionaries could wish for. For Pearse it was country of noble, honest, purposeful young men. For James Connolly it meant a collectivist socialist society. To others it meant a conservative Catholic land, of small farms and industry. Regardless, the idea of a Gaelic Ireland was to be extremely important in early 20th century Irish nationalism. Pearse, in a speech in 1915 declared, "Ireland must not only be free but Gaelic as well".

Cultural nationalism necessarily had political implications. People who met in Gaelic League Irish classes inevitably began to discuss (in English usually) nationalist political questions. If Ireland was a culture completely separate from Britain and if, in fact, its culture was actually being killed off by the imperial power, the next logical step was that to save Irish national identity, Ireland itself would have to separate completely from England. That many in the Gaelic League and the GAA reached this conclusion was no doubt in part due to the fact that IRB from the start infiltrated both organizations to recruit and proselytize.[32] From Gaelic League activism to leadership of the Easter Rising via the Volunteers came Patrick Pearse, Joseph Plunkett and Eamon de Valera among many others. All three only joined the IRB after joining the Volunteers in 1913–1914. Amongst many other rank and file militants were men such as Michael Collins, WT Cosgrave, Richard Mulcahy. The Gaelic League was also one of the few nationalist organizations where men and women mixed freely. The women's cultural nationalist organization was named Inghinidhe na hÉireann (Daughters of Ireland) and the parallel female equivalent of the Volunteers was known as Cumman na mBan (The League of Women).

If the Gaelic League formed the social and cultural background of separatist nationalism, its foremost political expression was Sinn Fein ("Ourselves") founded in Dublin by Arthur Griffith in 1905.

Griffith argued in a book titled *The Resurrection of Hungary* that Irish nationalists should model their search for independence on that of Hungary. There, elected representatives had seceded from the Austrian Habsburg parliament and set up their own parliament under the sovereignty of the Habsburg monarch. They had thus been recognized as equal parts of the "Dual Monarchy". In the same way, Irish MPs should withdraw from Westminster and declare an Irish Parliament in existence. If necessary, after a campaign of passive, though not armed, resistance Ireland could be an equal but separate part of a Windsor "Dual Monarchy". Sinn Fein's economic policy was based on making Ireland self-sufficient and the promotion of Irish industry. If Griffith's embrace of monarchy over republicanism was to have little future in Irish nationalist circles, his advocacy of using elected representatives as a means of unilaterally declaring independence was largely to become reality in 1918–19. In 1916, however, all this lay in the future. At the time, Sinn Fein had no MPs and a handful of county councillors, mostly in Dublin city, where it had only 4 out of 80 seats.[33] It had no explicit links with the IRB, though there was some crossover in membership. Nevertheless, because of the party's public profile, all separatists of the era were popularly referred to as "Sinn Feiners".[34] Thus, although the Sinn Fein Party took no part in the Rising, it was commonly named the "Sinn Fein Rebellion".

There was one final strand of in the militant separatist movement. This was the very recent phenomenon of Irish socialist republicanism. Alongside the 1,000 or so Volunteers who took part in the Easter Rising were 200 or so men and women from the Irish Citizen Army. The Citizen Army was, like the Volunteers, an open, uniformed and armed body. It had been formed in November 1913, just before the Volunteers in fact, but in very different circumstances.

Originally it had emerged from the Irish Transport and General Workers' Union and had been a trade union militia, designed to protect striking workers from police aggression. It was born during a protracted and bitter industrial dispute known to history as the Dublin Lockout in 1913–14. The Lockout represents to the Irish Labour movement almost as potent a symbol as the Easter Rising does to Irish republicans – involving as it did a nascent trade union movement (the ITGWU was founded only in 1908), and 20,000 workers, taking on the Dublin business establishment over the right to be represented in the union of their choice. The dispute – in which a consortium of employers, led by William Martin Murphy, owner of the Dublin United Tramway Company and the Independent Group of newspapers tried to enforce an oath in which workers would swear not join the militant ITGWU – was both intensely fought and extremely violent. Strikers physically attacked Murphy's trams and his "scabs", beating to death at least two in the course of the dispute. The police, both the Dublin Metropolitan Police and the RIC, baton-charged union rallies, and even made sorties into the slum buildings to beat up strikers there – accounting for at least two more deaths. The employers even handed over revolvers to strike-breakers for self protection, resulting in several fatal shootings of strikers. The Citizen Army, therefore, was at first simply a self-defence organization as well as a way of keeping those out of work during the strike busy – drilling in the ITGWU's sports grounds with bats and hurling sticks.

That it became a revolutionary, armed cadre was essentially down to the influence of one man, its leader James Connolly. Connolly was born in Edinburgh of Irish parentage.

Connolly – who had worked variously as a soldier in the British Army, a carter and finally as trade union organizer, principally in Dublin and Belfast – was self-educated and a convinced Marxist. His ideology was a mixture of traditional Irish republicanism and socialism, which he had elaborated in a short book titled *Labour in Irish History*. The two must have sat awkwardly with each other at times. In the Lockout for example, his "class enemy" William Martin Murphy, was a Catholic and a former Nationalist MP, whereas the strikers depended heavily on financial support from sympathetic unions in Britain. For Connolly, "only the Irish working class remain as the incorruptible inheritors of the fight for Irish freedom".[35] His argument was that bourgeois Irish nationalists were too tied into the British Imperial capitalist economy to be truly separatist. At the same time, the British Empire would never allow social revolution to take place in Ireland, hence "The cause of Labour is the cause of Ireland, the cause of Ireland is the cause of Labour".[36] To provide context, it should be stated that Connolly lived and worked in a world of oppressive poverty in the Dublin slums. Connolly had founded a political party, the Irish Socialist Republican Party in the 1890s but it had never got off the ground.

In 1914, with the departure of Jim Larkin, the founder and leader of the ITGWU to America, Connolly found himself at the head of the union and of its militia, the Citizen Army. With the aid of another former soldier, Michael Mallin, he had armed, uniformed and trained the small force – the only nationalist military grouping to have equal status for men and women. By late 1915 it was preparing for insurrection against British rule.

The rebels of Easter 1916 were therefore a rather mixed bunch. A secret society of republican conspirators, an open (though heavily infiltrated) armed nationalist militia and a fair scattering of cultural and linguistic nationalists, along with a small, though well-organized, socialist labour element. All of these groups had their reasons for wanting Ireland to be free of the British Empire, but why did they choose to try and achieve this though armed insurrection? Political violence was not unknown in early 20th century Ireland – indeed the country was a lot more violent then than later in the century. Politically-motivated violence came in several forms. There was state violence: for example, the British Army's shootings at Bachelor's Walk in 1914. There was also sectarian violence: several died in rioting between Catholics and Protestants in Belfast, where knives and revolvers were used, in July 1912.[37] Social and agrarian violence claimed lives too, as in the Lockout in Dublin and in the west, where the RIC reported county Galway to be "disturbed" in 1914. And finally there was intra-nationalist or party-political violence. The Irish Parliamentary Party had not one, but two strong-arm organizations – the United Irish League and the Ancient Order of Hibernians – and in Cork city, 11 eleven people were shot, two fatally, in elections in 1910 and 1914, in confrontations with the rival nationalist All For Ireland League.[38]

But the Easter Rising was violence of a whole new character and intensity. This was revolutionary violence, designed to challenge the state and if possible topple it. Home Rule, albeit delayed, was on the British statute books. Why not just wait for self-government and proceed from there? Why did the Easter Rising take place and inaugurate a prolonged period of armed conflict in Ireland? There is one easy answer to this question and a second more difficult one. The first answer is that many nationalists in 1916 did not believe that Home Rule was really going to come to pass. The Ulster Volunteers' mobilization and the refusal of the British military to act against them in 1913–14 demonstrated to some that armed force was the only thing that guaranteed political change in Ireland.

The second reason is more subtle. The separatists in their various forms wanted an independent Ireland – not Home Rule. They also felt almost an obligation to fight "England" to get it. Desmond Fitzgerald, a 1916 rebel, said that if a Rising was not launched before the end of the First World War, "Irish nationality would flicker out": "The reaction of the Irish people after the declaration of war filled me with the conviction that we had reached a point where the Irish people were accepted completely their absorption by the British". If that happened, "it would be futile to talk of ourselves other than as inhabitants of that part of England that used to be called Ireland. In that state of mind I had decided that extreme action must be taken".[39] It was as if it was only through revolutionary fighting for Ireland that one could become truly Irish. Irish identity was something many radical nationalists felt was under threat and the sight of thousands of Irishmen serving in the British Army in the European War to them spelt its death-knell. Armed conflict with the British Empire, "striking a blow for freedom" was therefore not only a political tactic but also a way of, "reviving" and "redeeming" Irish nationality by defining it in armed struggle against the British state.

Part IV: Planning the Rising

The Easter Rising was very much the product of the First World War. First of all, the war streamlined the Volunteers into a separatist core. When John Redmond committed the Volunteers to backing the British War effort, the movement split. Redmond and his appointees were purged from the Volunteers' command by the disgusted separatists, but most of the rank and file followed Redmond, who took 142,000 men into a new National Volunteer organization.[40] Only around 9,700 stayed with the original group. The split was acrimonious, but unlike many others in Irish nationalist history, bloodless. The two sides would abuse each in the press but they parted ways and even divided weapons by mutual agreement. Moreover, for those within the Volunteers who were committed to armed struggle, the split was not an altogether unwelcome development as it pared down the Volunteers into a much more homogenous and politically committed force.

Shortly after the War broke out, a small cabal within both the Volunteers and the IRB, behind of the backs of both organizations' leaders, began to plan an insurrection, to take place before the war was over. In early 1915, the group was formalized into the "Military Committee". Connolly, who since the war had started was writing belligerent articles about armed rebellion in his newspaper, the *Irish Worker*, was co-opted onto the Committee in early 1915. It was this group, a conspiracy within a conspiracy, that was to plan the Rising. Eoin MacNeill and Bulmer Hobson, respectively heads of the Volunteers and the IRB were kept in ignorance of the plot until virtually the last minute. MacNeill's position was that the Volunteers should be kept armed and trained until Home Rule was passed, but that they should not confront the state unless the British either tried to suppress nationalist organizations or impose conscription on Ireland. Hobson, similarly, was against a resort to arms unless the majority of the population was behind it, a stance that was actually laid down by the IRB's constitution.

The military plan, composed by George Plunkett, was kept so secret that no record of it has survived, but so far as historians have been able to reconstruct it, it was this. The main body of Volunteers were to seize central Dublin and also its main port at Kingstown (now Dun Laoighaire). There they were to hold out for as long as possible and await reinforcements from the surrounding counties. In the west, the plan issued to Volunteers in Galway, Clare and Limerick was to hold, "the line of the Shannon" and keep the British garrisons there pinned west of it. The thinking was that if re-taking Ireland could be made very costly for the British, they might prefer to negotiate rather than divert major resources from the Great War's Western Front.

The plan was, apparently, based on Robert Emmet's blueprint of 1803. One Volunteer saw Thomas MacDonagh poring over a copy of Emmet's original plan shortly before the Rising.[41] This all sounds hopelessly unrealistic for a poorly armed militia of 10,000 or so men. Admittedly the Germans had promised arms to the insurgents, via Roger Casement (an Ulster Protestant and former British diplomat turned radical separatist). Small arms alone in the hands of amateur soldiers could not hope to defeat the British military. However, there was a secondary objective. Connolly wrote, "if the British use artillery in Dublin they are doomed".[42] He may have had a point. If British rule could be reduced to the use of blunt physical force to put down a nationalist rebellion, it would be fatally compromised in the eyes of Catholic and nationalist Ireland. Irish people would have to choose between British repression and Irish insurgents. In such a scenario, the willingness to compromise that underpinned the politics of Home Rule and the Irish Parliamentary Party would be swept away.

The World War and the demands it forced the British state to make of its citizens put it in a most dangerous position in Ireland. Mathew Nathan, the Under Secretary for Ireland, thought that Redmond, the Parliamentary leader, had not carried his constituency with him. Although recruitment for the War in Ireland was reasonable, it was only about two thirds of that in Britain itself. Moreover, as the war went on and casualties mounted, it fell sharply and even from very early on in the war, the idea of conscription was deeply unpopular in Ireland. One contemporary writer thought that "behind it all was the vague feeling that to fight for the British Empire was disloyal to Ireland".[43] Catholic Irish people might sometimes identified with the empire – future IRA leader Ernie O'Malley and his brothers got into a fist fight with some Volunteers who tried to snatch their union jack-coloured horns at a recruiting rally in 1914.[44] The problem was, as O'Malley himself was to show, they could not be relied on. As early as November 1915, with no end to the war in sight and with Home Rule still not enacted, British sources were reporting signs of disaffection. Also in 1915, the Catholic Church turned against the war and recruitment.

Against this background, the Volunteers, Citizen Army (and also a small group called the Hibernian rifles), trained and paraded intensively. Although the plans for the Rising were the work of a small closed group, they do not seem to have misled the rank and file, who by and large, were eager to fight. In the lead up to the Rising, Volunteer companies were put to work making improvised hand grenades, so it seems most unlikely they did not know that action of some kind was imminent. They were, in 1914–1915, a regular sight on the streets of Dublin, uniformed in dark green and armed with rifles. On St Patrick's Day 1916, they staged a mock insurrection in central Dublin, including an "attack" on Dublin Castle, without any intervention by the police or military.

With hindsight it seems almost astonishing that the British allowed an armed and openly hostile nationalist group to parade and manoeuvre in full view on the streets of the Irish capital. Even more so, given that they knew from intercepted telegraphs from America to Berlin that the Volunteers, via John Devoy and Clan na Gael in the US, were in contact with and had been offered help by the Germans.[45]

In fact there was fierce debate on this point within the British administration. Birrell the Chief Secretary and Nathan, the Under Secretary were of the opinion that clamping down on the radical nationalist groups would be more politically costly than it was worth and would alienate the broad nationalist community. The Lord Lieutenant, Wimborne, on the other hand and British military intelligence argued insistently that "seditious" groups must be disarmed. However, in the event, despite having extensive emergency powers under the wartime Defence of the Realm

25

Act (DORA), the British state in Ireland was only intermittently repressive. Connolly's *Irish Worker*, for example was closed down for "seditious language" but only weeks later was replaced with the almost identical *Workers Republic*. A number of IRB activists, notably Ernest Blythe, were arrested and deported for anti-recruitment agitation. On the whole though, the Volunteers were largely left alone in the months before the Rising.

Birrell's policy was naturally fiercely criticized after the rebellion, but was it really as misguided as it seems? Birrell was a highly experienced and not unsympathetic observer of Irish nationalist politics. He knew that Irish self-rule was coming in some form and in the meantime, keeping a semi-loyal population in line under a liberal democratic system needed a soft touch. Repression would therefore be counter-productive by alienating a much broader constituency than the separatists themselves.[46] Piaras Beaslai, in 1916 an IRB man and Volunteer, thought Birrell was in fact, one the biggest problems they faced. "As one who was working tooth and nail to bring about an insurrection, I can testify that one of the biggest obstacles was the cleverness of Mr. Birrell's policy".[47]

There is even a suggestion that elements of the British state allowed the Rising to happen so they could put down the Volunteers. Just before the Rising, British military intelligence intercepted a telegram to Berlin giving the date and location of the rebellion. Whether or not Birrell and the Dublin Castle administration were informed we do not know.[48] What we can be sure of though, is that despite ample warning of what was about to happen, the Rising caught the British totally unprepared.

Part V: The Brink

Two dramatic events immediately preceded the insurrection. One was the near landing of the German arms for the Volunteers, along with Roger Casement. The other was the revelation, at the last minute, of the imminent rebellion to the leaders of the Volunteers and the IRB.

The Germans had placed only a low priority on the aid to rebels in Ireland. What they sent was very much second-rate weaponry, captured from the Russians in 1914. Nevertheless, it was substantial. Aboard a ship named the *Aud* were 10,000 rifles, 10 machine guns and thousands of rounds of ammunition. To put this into perspective, the Volunteers had at most 5,000 or so weapons in their possession in the whole country, and many of these were of obsolete patterns.[49] The *Aud* narrowly avoided several British patrol ships and convinced others that it was Norwegian trawler. It anchored off Fenit in Kerry for hours waiting for the local Volunteers to respond to their signals. In the meantime, it attracted the attention of British vessels in the area, who pursued it into Cork harbour. Realizing the game was up, the ship's captain scuttled the vessel and its weaponry.

A party of five Volunteers, sent by car from Dublin to try and contact the ship, drove, in pitch darkness over the pier at Banna Strand, drowning three of them. They were the first casualties of the Rising. The following day a U-boat landed Roger Casement nearby at Fenit. Casement, who had tried in vain both to raise a

Volunteer unit from Irish prisoners of war held by the Germans (he got only 55 recruits) and to persuade the Germans themselves to send an expedition to Ireland, intended to try and stop the Rising, which he was convinced would be a bloody failure. Before he could do anything, however, he was arrested by a suspicious policeman.[50] He would be hanged in August for treason. The loss of the German arms shipment was a major blow to the prospects of the rebellion – especially outside of Dublin. Even with the arms, the prospect of a nationwide rebellion was a long shot. Without them it would be all but impossible.

On the 21st of April 1916, Volunteer companies around the country were informed that they would parade with full kit on Easter Sunday, April 23. Only the Military Committee and the very restricted number of people they had told knew that this was actually the signal for rebellion. At the last minute, the leadership of the Volunteers and IRB were also informed. The IRB conspirators handled their nominal leaders more efficiently than the dissident Volunteers. Bulmer Hobson was kidnapped at gunpoint and held in a house in Dublin for the week. Some even wanted to shoot him. Dennis McCullough, President of The Organization, was more pliable: he reluctantly agreed to go along with the rebellion.

Eoin MacNeill, chief of the Volunteers, was another matter however. He was summoned to a house in suburban Dublin and told bluntly that the rising was to go ahead the following day, with or without his consent. Pearse told him petulantly "we don't need you any more", and walked out. MacNeill though, an academic and independent thinker, very nearly stopped the event in its tracks. He took out an advertisement in the Sunday Independent which advised the

Volunteers that, "all manoeuvres for today are cancelled".[51] Micheal O'Rahilly (known as "The O'Rahilly" in separatist circles) drove around through the country, in a frenetic two-day period, trying to enforce the countermanding order. In the event, MacNeill and O'Rahilly's efforts only postponed the Rising for a day. The Military Committee managed to get word to reliable units that the "manoeuvres" would be going ahead on Monday instead. O'Rahilly himself quixotically joined the Rising, and would die in it.

In the meantime, MacNeill's order caused almost indescribable chaos among Volunteer units around the country. Sean MacEntee, commander of the Volunteers in Louth, sent a contingent south to seize the RIC barracks in the village of Ardee, only to get word on the Sunday that the Rising had been cancelled. He had to send three messengers after them on bicycle before he managed to halt the column. Finally having caught up with his men on Monday, he got further information that the rebellion was actually going ahead. MacEntee ended up cycling to Dublin from Drogheda, all through the night, through sheets of pouring rain to get confirmation. Having eventually met his superiors, he got back to Louth in time to discover that most of his men had dispersed. He finished the week in Dublin, where he fought in the GPO.[52]

MacNeill's "countermanding order" has often been blamed for the Rising being confined to Dublin. No doubt there is some truth in this. In Cork, for example, around 1,000 Volunteers were ready on Easter Sunday – as many as in Dublin – but they went home after receiving a string of contradictory orders from the capital.[53] On the other hand, in the absence of sufficient arms and coherent planning there was little enough the rebels in the provinces could have done anyway. In county Galway, where up to 700 men took part in the Rising, a large but poorly-armed contingent (they had only 25 rifles) roamed the countryside for several days before dispersing when faced with British reinforcements.[54] In county Wexford, the Volunteers took over Enniscorthy for a week, but again, capitulated without a shot being fired towards the end of the week.[55] It is, therefore more than likely that the serious fighting of Easter week would have happened in Dublin – the centre of Volunteer organization and weaponry – regardless of MacNeill's order. In Dublin itself, the countermand cost the Rising some manpower, but perhaps not as much as is sometimes claimed. On St Patrick's Day that year, 1,400 men Volunteers mobilized for exercises in Dublin – where they occupied the city centre for an hour. In the actual rebellion, about a month later, only slightly fewer men – 1,200 or so – fought in the Rising.[56] For the most part the delay simply meant a day of nerve-jangling waiting and a sleepless night for Dublin Volunteers.

Early on Monday morning April 24, 1916, the Volunteers and Citizen Army assembled at various points in Dublin, marched out and took over pre-appointed strong-points in the city centre. The Rising had begun.

Part VI: The Rising

On Easter Monday, James Stephens – a writer, nationalist and registrar of the National Gallery in Dublin – started hearing strange rumours. There had been rifle firing in the city all day. Returning from lunch to his office, he encountered a crowd of onlookers at Stephen's Green:

> "Has there been an accident?" said I, "What's all this for"? A sleepy rough-looking man answered, "Don't you know? The Sinn Feiners have seized the city this morning". "Oh", said I... "They seized the city at eleven o'clock this morning. The Green there is full of them. They have captured the Castle, they have taken the Post Office". "My God", said I staring at him, and turned and went running towards the Green... I saw the gates were closed and men were standing inside with guns on their shoulders.[57]

Ernie O'Malley, then a medical student, was strolling through Dublin, it was a bank holiday and he had the day off. On O'Connell Street (or Sackville Street as it then was) he saw

> large groups of people gathered together. From the flagstaff on top of the General Post Office, the GPO, floated a new flag, a tricoloured one of green, white and orange... "What's it all about?" I asked a man who stood near me, a scowl on his face. "Those boyhoes the Volunteers have seized the Post Office, they want

nothing less than a Republic", he laughed scornfully...
On the base of [Nelson's] Pillar there was a white poster.
Gathered around it were groups of men and women.
Some looked at it with serious faces, some laughed and
sniggered. I began to read it with a smile but my smile
ceased as I read, POBLACHT NA H EIREANN,
THE PROVISIONAL GOVERNMENT OF THE
IRISH REPUBLIC.[58]

There were some dead horses lying on the street, testament to a
skirmish between the Volunteers and a troop of British cavalry,
"Those fellows" O'Malley was told, "are not going to be frightened
by a troop of lancers. They mean business."[59]

Dubliners woke up on Monday morning and suddenly found the
city centre occupied by armed men (and some women) in a mixture
of dark green uniforms and civilian clothes. James Connolly had
mobilized the main body at Liberty Hall, the Transport Union's
headquarters. He was in command of the men O'Malley saw, who
took over the GPO and most of Sackville Street. Also north of
the Liffey, Volunteers under Ned Daly took over the Four Courts,
the centre of the Irish legal system, and the clump of little streets
behind it. The men Stephens encountered on Stephen's Green were
mostly Citizen Army men, commanded by Michael Mallin. Most
unwisely, they dug in on the Green, which was overlooked by high
buildings on every side. Several hundred metres away, another
body of Volunteers under Thomas MacDonagh had occupied
Jacob's Biscuit Factory on Aungier Street. Further to the west, there
were two main Volunteer strong-points, one in the South Dublin
Union, a vast complex of workhouses and hospitals on the site of

present day James' Hospital, under the command of Eamon Ceant, the other in Jameson's Distillery at Marrowbone Lane, overlooking the Grand Canal. Finally, at the other end of the canal to the south-east was a garrison led by Eamon de Valera, ensconced in Boland's Mill. A detachment of this force guarded the canal crossing at Mount Street Bridge and another covered the military barracks at Beggar's Bush.

Dublin's old centre can be imagined as an elongated oval, like a misshapen rugby ball, bisected by the river Liffey, which runs from one end of the oval to the other. Its perimeters are bounded by two canals, the Royal on the north side and the Grand to the south. Running roughly parallel to the canals are two Circular roads, again North and South. This was the area the insurgents wanted to hold. However, in 1916, this district was abutted by no less than five British Army barracks, three around the southern rim of the oval along the Grand Canal, another at Kilmainham, at the oval's western point and one more, just beyond the Four Courts on the river Liffey. Broadly speaking, with the exception of the headquarters at the GPO, the Volunteers' positions had been chosen as defensive sites against a counter attack from these barracks.

However, strategically speaking, there were some major flaws. The rebels had left two imposing and highly symbolic buildings in British hands, right in the centre both of the city and of their positions. Dublin Castle, the centre of British rule, and Trinity College. The Castle had been attacked by a small party of Citizen Army fighters, but, after shooting a policeman, they had found the gates locked and retired to the rooftop of the adjacent City Hall, from where they exchanged shots with rapidly arriving British reinforcements. No attempt was made to take Trinity, the Protestant and largely Unionist University, which stood right in the path between the rebel garrisons north and south of the Liffey. A scratch force of armed students was put together to defend it, and as the week went on, further British forces were funnelled in. Just as seriously, the Volunteers failed to take or put out of action either of Dublin's two train stations – at Amiens Street (now Connolly Station) and Kingsbridge (now Heuston Station) which the British would use to bring in reinforcements from their garrisons in The Curragh and Belfast. Finally, while some of the bridges over the canal – at Marrowbone Lane and Mount Street particularly – were strongly held, others were not manned at all. The result was that instead of a compact city centre stronghold, the insurgents ultimately found themselves in isolated positions which had to withstand British counter-attacks more or less alone. By the end of the week, communications between the rebel posts were only kept open by the odd Cumman na mBan (female) messenger who braved the hostile areas in between.

For most of Dublin's citizens, the rising was a bolt out of the blue, and from the civilians the Volunteers at first experienced utter incomprehension and not a little hostility. Ernie O'Malley recalled the reaction of people in his middle-class neighbourhood:

> The loyalists spoke with an air of contempt, "the troops will settle the matter in an hour or two, these pro-Germans will run away"... The Redmondites were more bitter, "I hope they'll all be hanged"... "Shooting's too good for them. Trying to stir up trouble for us all."[60]

In the working-class areas of Sackville street, Jacob's factory and the South Dublin Union, many people had dependents serving in the British Army in the Great War. Wives of soldiers were paid 'separation money', and these women were bitterly hostile to the insurrection. O'Malley heard women abusing the Volunteers outside the GPO: "you dirty bowsies, wait till the Tommies bate yer bloody heads off"; "If only my Johnny was back from the front you'd be running with your bloody well tail between your legs."[61]

Elsewhere the Volunteers had occupied places of work and welfare (such as there were) of poor working-class people. In several cases the rebels had to use force against the locals to occupy their positions. At Jacob's factory, a Volunteer named Sean Murphy recalled, "some civilians had... attacked one of the Volunteers and in order to save his life they had to shoot one of the civilians".[62] At South Dublin Union, the Volunteers found themselves involved in a riot with locals and had to "lay out" two with rifle butts before they got into the complex.[63] At Stephen's Green, the Citizen Army had seized passing cars and carts at gunpoint to serve as barricades. James Stephens saw a carter try to remove his livelihood from the barricades, only to be shot dead by the insurgents. "At that moment the Volunteers were hated."[64]

If the initial civilian reaction was one of bewilderment, the British were almost equally astonished. Many of their officers had been at the Races in Fairyhouse and there were only around 1,000 troops left in the city.[65] Lord Wimborne, the Lord Lieutenant, his worst fears having come to pass, declared martial law and handed over power to General Lowe.[66] If nothing else, the rebellion had at least freed him to clamp down on "sedition" – as he had been recommending for months. On the first day of the Rising, there were, by and large, only brushes between the Volunteers and the British military. Two troops of British cavalry, sent out to investigate the strange happenings were badly shot up on O'Connell Street and on the quays in front of the Four Courts. A bomb was detonated at the Army's arms dump in Phoenix Park, failing to destroy the arsenal but killing an unfortunate bystander.[67] On Mount Street, a group of reserve volunteer soldiers, nicknamed in Dublin, the "Gorgeous Wrecks" (because of their advanced age and their tunics' inscriptions 'Georgius Rex'), unwittingly stumbled upon the rebel position and four were killed before they scrambled into safety at Beggars Bush barracks.[68]

In fact, had the rebels known of the weakness of the British garrison, they could have taken such important points as Dublin Castle (garrisoned by only seven soldiers[69]), Trinity College (no garrison) and Beggars Bush (held initially by the army catering staff and 17 rifles[70]) with relative ease. Only at South Dublin Union, which was attacked by troops from the adjacent Kilmainham barracks, was there serious fighting on the first day, and there the British command ordered a halt until they had come to terms with what they were dealing with.

Three of the unarmed Dublin Metropolitan Police were shot on the first day of the Rising and their Commissioner pulled them off the streets. The decision, though understandable, unleashed an orgy of looting, especially around Sackville Street, as slum dwellers from the surrounding area took the once-in-a-lifetime opportunity to ransack the city's shops and boutiques.[71] According to one onlooker, "a horrible procession poured into the streets, mainly women and girls... they started with sticks and stones, a breach would be made [in a shop], the door would be forced in", if the shopkeeper resisted, "they would beat him and down him without mercy". A total of 425 people were arrested after the Rising for looting.[72] The Volunteers tried but largely failed to keep order and were reduced to shooting over the heads of looters to try and disperse them. So, sitting in mostly disconnected positions, with a civilian population at best ambivalent, at worst downright hostile, the Volunteers awaited the British counterattack.

Most Dubliners expected the Rising to be crushed within hours and were very surprised when it was not. In fact it took several days for the British military machine to rumble clumsily into action. Reinforcements arrived from the Military depot at the Curragh, clambered off the train at Amiens Street from Belfast and landed at the port in Kingstown (Dun Laoghaire). General Lowe had only 1,600 troops under his command on Tuesday, but had 16,000 men in the city by the Friday, backed up by field artillery rushed from Athlone and a gunboat, the *Helga*, which sailed down the Liffey.[73] Effectively, the British would suffocate the Rising with overwhelming force. Nevertheless, the task proved far from straightforward. Lowe's first move was to open a line of communication along the river Liffey and to throw a cordon of troops around the Volunteers' strongholds.

Where the rebels sat in fixed positions, as at the GPO, they were steadily isolated and bombarded into surrender. When James Stephens returned to Stephen's Green on the Tuesday, he found it littered with dead and wounded Volunteers, caught by fire from the surrounding buildings. The insurgents there retreated to the College of Surgeons, where they remained for the rest of the week.[74] The neighbouring Jacob's factory saw little fighting, as did Boland's Mill and the Four Courts.

The Volunteers' headquarters at the GPO took the brunt of the British artillery bombardment. Much of O'Connell Street was reduced to burning rubble and the GPO itself became an inferno. James Stephens, observing the blaze from his window, wrote, "I saw a red flare that crept to the sky and stole over it and remained there glaring; the smoke reached from the ground to the clouds, and I could see great red sparks go soaring to enormous heights; while always in the calm air there was the buzzing thudding and rattling of guns".[75]

Inside the building were the Rising's principal leaders, James Connolly and Patrick Pearse. Connolly, a former soldier, was a whirlwind of activity, building barricades, issuing orders and scouting the surrounding positions. On Thursday, while on Abbey street, he was badly wounded in the leg by a ricochet. He was treated by a captured British medic and then carried on a stretcher back to the firing line, where he kept himself occupied by reading a detective novel.[76] Pearse, the writer and educationalist, in the words of one participant, "sat out there in the front on one of the high stools, people would come up and talk to him".[77]

By Friday, the grand buildings of Dublin, having burned fiercely for two days, were crashing down around them. A sortie led by O'Rahily tried to break out of the GPO but was shot up badly – 21 out of 30 men were hit by fire from the ever closer British barricades. O'Rahily himself was killed and lay sprawled, face up, on Henry Street in full view of his comrades. The survivors, led by Pearse and Plunkett, tunneled through the walls of adjacent buildings and escaped the blazing Post Office into the little streets around Moore Street.

Elsewhere, the thick walls of the rebels' positions usually protected them from British shells and bullets, but the psychological strain of waiting, inactive, for the British counter-attack proved excruciating. In Boland's Mill, Eamon de Valera refused to sleep for six nights, pacing furiously up and down the post. He ordered nearby Westland Row railway station to be burnt, only to change his mind and have his men then put out the fire. One volunteer cracked under the pressure and shot one of his comrades before being clubbed down. Nevertheless, the garrison there was spared coming under direct shell-fire due to a brainwave of de Valera's. He had a tricolour flown on a neighbouring, empty building, which the British obligingly pounded with artillery.[78]

Where, however, the British assaulted Volunteer positions dominating the routes into the city, fighting was much more bloody. There they were drawn into street fighting, with its invisible snipers and sudden close range cross-fires, which negated their superiority in men and firepower. This happened mainly at three locations, Mount Street Bridge, South Dublin Union/Marrowbone Lane and North King Street.

At Mount Street, on the approach to the city centre from the port at Kingstown, a Volunteer outpost manned by only 17 men, armed with rifles and handguns, inflicted 240 casualties on attacking British troops.[79] The rebels occupied the stately Clanwilliam House – commanding the crossing over the Grand Canal – and two houses on Northumberland road, an upper class, leafy, red-bricked neighbourhood. They were faced by a British regiment, the Sherwood Foresters, just off the boat from a training depot in England, and so inexperienced that they had to be shown on the pier at Kingstown how to fire and reload their weapons.[80] On top of that, they had left behind their grenades and their Lewis machine guns had been lost in the crossing.[81] Marching up through the suburbs, they were warmly applauded by the crowds still enjoying the Spring Show at the Royal Dublin Society, until they stumbled into the crossfire at Northumberland Road. Ten were hit in the first attack.[82] Although there was an alternative crossing of the canal available just a street away at Baggot Street, which would have flanked the Volunteers' position, General Lowe ordered that the bridge at Mount Street be taken "at all costs".[83] For the rest of the day, at the sound of whistles every twenty minutes, waves of hapless troops, led by officers with drawn swords, charged up the Road, only to be shot down.

By the evening, the road was carpeted with dead and wounded British troops, many moaning in pain and trying feebly to drink from their water bottles. The survivors crawled into the gutters and doorways at either side of the road for some cover, while others huddled under a low wall at the canal. For the Volunteers, despite the hopeless odds, it was exhilarating. Inside Clanwilliam House, two Volunteers, Patrick Doyle and Tom Walsh, shouted over the noise of battle, "Isn't this a great day for Ireland?" "Isn't it that?", "Did I ever think I'd see a fight like this? Shouldn't we all be grateful to the good God that he has allowed us to take part in a fight like this?" No sooner were the words out of Doyle's mouth when he was hit in the head and killed.[84] De Valera, with over a hundred fighters, was only two streets away in Boland's Mill, but his command never reinforced the Volunteers at Mount Street. Eventually, on the Thursday, the position was stormed when the British brought up machine guns and explosives. Four Volunteers were killed and another captured. The rest slipped away. The fighting there had inflicted up to two thirds of British casualties in Easter week.[85]

The British never took the Volunteer positions at South Dublin Union and Marrowbone Lane which blocked the route into town from the southwest. They attacked it on Thursday and ferocious close-quarter fighting took place in the hospitals and workhouses. The British troops had to fight for every building, in wards where patients still lay as bullets and grenades flew around them. The Volunteers, too few to hold the whole complex, made their stronghold in the nurses' building. A determined charge of British troops broke into it, only to find the inside of the building barricaded. Volleys of rifle fire and grenades were exchanged at point blank range. Cathal Brugha at one point held the barricade alone, badly wounded by a grenade blast, until the other Volunteers in the building heard him singing and came back to help him.

The British soldiers, who were no less raw recruits than the Sherwood Foresters who had been massacred on Mount Street the day before, were the first to break off the nightmarish, claustrophobic combat – retreating to the Union bakery. From there they and the Volunteers eyed each other until Sunday.[86] In the Jameson Distillery on Marrowbone Lane, right beside the Union complex, the British made several unsuccessful frontal assaults from over the canal. Volunteer Robert Holland was put in a top floor room with a Cumman na mBan woman, who loaded his two rifles while he fired. By Thursday evening, he "could see quite a lot of [British soldiers'] bodies all around outside the wall and as far as Dolphins Barn Bridge. I could just see a pit and Red Cross men working at it putting bodies into it".[87]

The rebel position around North King Street straddled the route towards the GPO along the north side of the river Liffey. It was only about ten minutes' walk from the GPO, in a mesh of little streets and tenements behind the Four Courts. Ned Daly's Volunteers had barricaded each of the streets and it was here that the most vicious street fighting of the week occurred. At close range, death was waiting around every corner, from behind every chimney and behind every barricade. Starting on Thursday, the British tried to smother the enclave. Mostly they avoided direct fire by tunnelling through the walls of the slum houses. A platoon that made a bayonet charge on one of the barricades was blasted by heavy Mauser bullets; the Volunteers scrambled over the barricade to take arms and ammunition from the dead and wounded.[88]

By the end of the week, the area was still not cleared. It was also here that the worst atrocity of the Rising took place. The South Staffordshire regiment, under a colonel Taylor, advanced in two days 150 yards down North King Street, losing 11 dead and 28 wounded. Infuriated, they broke into the homes of the locals and shot or bayoneted 15 civilian men whom they accused of being rebels.[89] Ellen Walsh, a resident of Mount Street recalled soldiers pounding on her door until she opened, and demanding, "Are there any men in this house?" Thirty soldiers ransacked the house, "like wild animals or things possessed". They took the two men in the house aside, one of them Walsh's husband, and killed them.[90]

On Friday the 28th of April, Pearse issued orders to surrender. The remnants of his command from the GPO were cornered in and around Moore Street. O'Rahily was dead, Connolly was badly wounded – his leg wound had turned gangrenous. There was talk of trying to break through to Daly's men around the Four Courts but it proved to be no more than that. In reality the Volunteers and Citizen Army men were tightly ringed by British rifles, machine guns and artillery on all sides. Three elderly civilians who tried to escape from Moore street towards the British barricades were swept away by a storm of bullets from the barricade in front of Pearse's eyes. It was this, apparently that moved him to surrender. He sent a tersely written note, via a Cumman na mBan nurse named Elizabeth O'Farrell, stating he wished to surrender, to "prevent the further slaughter of the civilian population and in the hope of saving our followers, now hopelessly surrounded and outnumbered".[91]

Pearse's surrender came late on Friday afternoon. The survivors of the GPO garrison emerged blinking from their Moore Street enclave and assembled at Nelson's Pillar, where they piled their arms and were marched to captivity in Richmond Barracks. Word still had to be got to the other rebel strongholds, however, none of which had yet been taken by the British. Elizabeth O'Farrell, accompanied by a priest, volunteered to bring the news to the Volunteers around the city.

At first, many of them didn't believe her. De Valera sent her away and had to be persuaded by officers who knew her she was genuine. Thomas MacDonagh in Jacob's factory thought the British had forged the note or forced Pearse to sign. In Marrowbone Lane, full with over 100 Volunteers and Cumman na mBan women, the rebels were convinced they were winning and had organized a victory *ceilidhe* (Irish dancing) for that night.[92] James Stephens was clear that despite the surrender at Moore Street, the insurrection was still not over on Saturday: "there is much rifle fire, but no sound from the machine guns, 18 pounders or trench mortars".[93]

It was Sunday the 30th before the last rebel garrisons, at South Dublin Union and Marrowbone Lane reluctantly surrendered.[94] Frank Robbins, a Citizen Army man, left an evocative account of the surrender in the College of Surgeons: "the act of surrender was a greater calamity than death itself. Men and women were crying openly with arms around each other's shoulders." It was only when British troops arrived that they recovered their composure: "we had nothing to be ashamed of." They might have failed, but as "others had failed before and they had not been ashamed or afraid of the consequences, why should we be?"[95]

Some rebel commanders like Joe McGrath at Marrowbone Lane told his men to escape – and did so himself with a "Toor a loo boys, I'm off".[96] Michael Mallin, the Citizen Army commander, also told anyone who thought they could escape to do so, as did John McBride in Jacob's factory, adding, if they ever got the chance to fight again, "don't get inside four walls".[97] De Valera on the other hand, insisted his men had to follow the surrender order to the letter, and they marched in formation into captivity.

Part of the popular memory of the Rising is that the Volunteers were pelted with abuse and missiles by hostile Dubliners as they marched under escort to prison. And there is no doubt that this did happen to some rebels. According to Max Caulfield's powerful description:

As the prisoners marched to Richmond Barracks, crowds stood at the kerbsides to hoot and jeer them. "Shoot the traitors!" they cried. "Bayonet the bastards!" In one of the poorer quarters the shawlies pelted them with rotten vegetables and the more enthusiastic disgorging the contents of their chamber pots over the beaten, yet somehow undefeated men.[98]

Similarly, Robert Holland, a Volunteer captured at the surrender of the South Dublin Union, remembered that as he was being marched to Richmond Barracks, "men, women and children used filthy expressions at us". Worst of all for Holland, a member of the Volunteer Company from the working class Inchicore, was that he knew many of his assailants. The prisoners "heard all of their names being called out at intervals by the bystanders. My name was called out by some boys and girls I had gone to school with... This was the first time I ever appreciated British troops, as they undoubtedly saved us from being manhandled that evening."[99]

This may not be the full story however. James Stephens thought that the mood in the city, though, "definitely anti-Volunteer", was more ambivalent. First of all, the people he talked to respected that the Volunteers, "are putting up a decent fight. For being beaten does not greatly matter in Ireland, but not fighting does matter. Had they been beaten on the first or second day, the city would have been humiliated to its soul." In general people had not yet taken sides:[100] "None of these people were prepared for Insurrection. The thing had been sprung on them so suddenly they were unable to take sides."[101]

A Dublin unionist, AM Bonaparte-Wyse, thought "the

sympathies of the ordinary Irish are with Sinn Fein."[102] Likewise, a Canadian journalist, FA McKenzie, found that, "in the poorer districts... there was a vast amount of sympathy with the rebels, particularly after the rebels were defeated."[103] The experience of Ernie O'Malley, the medical student who came upon the GPO takeover on Easter Monday was extreme. He actually joined in the fighting on the rebel side, sniping at British troops with a borrowed rifle and then helping fugitive Volunteers to get away after the surrender.[104]

At any rate, the Rising was over. General John Maxwell had arrived on Friday, just in time to take the surrender. He arrived in a burning city, with its main street in ruins. The fighting had cost the lives of 447 people and wounded 2,585. Of these, 116 were British soldiers, another 368 of whom were wounded. 16 policemen (13 RIC and three DMP) were killed. The British counted rebel and civilian casualties together, giving a total of 318 killed, 2,217 wounded. It was later ascertained that 62 of these were combatants – 50 Volunteers and 12 Citizen Army men.[105] Outside of Dublin, the only serious fighting had happened in county Meath, where the north Dublin Volunteers, unable to make their way into the city, had ambushed an RIC patrol at Ashbourne, killing 11 and taking over the Police barracks there.

Asquith, the British prime minister, said of the insurgents, "they conducted themselves with great humanity... they were misled I believe into this terrible business... [and] fought very bravely and without outrage".[106] The Volunteer prisoners equally had no animosity towards the ordinary British soldiers.[107]

However, if the combatants had "fought fair" and treated each other decently, the civilians had suffered from both sides. More than once on Easter Monday the Volunteers had shot civilians who got in their way. A great many of the civilian casualties were no doubt caught in the crossfire, and both the Volunteers and the British tried to move civilians out of danger in combat zones. However, in at least three separate incidents, British troops deliberately killed non-combatants.

The worst example was, as described above, in North King Street, where the soldiers had broken into houses and killed 15 men they found there. An inquiry was held, but it took no action against Colonel Taylor.[108] General Maxwell's conclusion was that such incidents "are absolutely unavoidable in such a business as this" and "responsibility for their deaths rests with those resisting His Majesty's troops in the execution of their duty."[109]

In Portobello barracks, an officer named Bowen Colthurst had murdered six civilians, including the pacifist, Francis Sheehy Skeffington, who had been trying to organize "citizen police" to stop the looting. When asked by British pickets if he was in sympathy with the Sinn Feiners, he most imprudently answered, "yes, but I am not in favour of militarism". He was taken to a cellar and shot.[110] Bowen Colthurst, described as "off his head" by his fellow officers was finally brought under control when a Major Vane arrived at the barracks, to find it surrounded by crowds shouting, "murderer".[111] A court martial was held but it found Bowen Colthurst insane and not liable for his actions.[112] A third case was that of a British sniper on a roof in Lower Mount Street who "went off his head and began to indiscriminately slaughter passers-by."[113]

Part VII: The Aftermath

In the burning GPO, Pearse wondered if they had done the right thing after all. "After a few years" he consoled himself, "people will see the meaning of what we tried to do."[114] What was amazing about the aftermath of the Rising is that the sea change in public opinion took only a few months. In the immediate aftermath, the Rising was condemned across the board in Ireland. Irish Party leader John Redmond said the rebels were his "irreconcilable enemies", who had "tried to torpedo Home Rule".[115] Within two years, Redmond and the Parliamentary Party would have sunk below a tide of sympathy for radical nationalism.

For this, the British response was largely to blame. Birrell and Nathan, the Chief Secretary and Deputy Chief Secretary, who had consistently refused to disarm the Volunteer movement on the grounds that it would antagonize the broad nationalist community, resigned. Their lenience was subsequently blamed for the Rising. General Maxwell, in the wake of the surrenders, declared martial law over all of Ireland. In a process of dubious legality, the leaders of the Rising were tried in secret and 15 shot in small batches over May 3–12. Pearse, Clarke and MacDonagh were the first to be shot, only four days after their surrender. One observer commented it was "like watching blood seep from behind a closed door." Connolly, badly wounded, had to be tied to a chair in order to face the firing squad. The British government intervened to commute the death sentences of another 90 rebels, including Eoin

MacNeill, before they could be shot.

Maxwell also sent mobile columns of cavalry, infantry and armoured cars throughout the country to disarm the Volunteers and arrest nationalist suspects. A total of 3,430 men and 70 women were rounded up.[116] The repression after the Rising was spread much further than the actual fighting. It was this that did much to inflame nationalist opinion against the British military. In Roscommon town, for example, (population 1,800) 700 troops arrived on May 7. They occupied the centre of town, sealed off the routes out and conducted a house-to-house search. 27 men were arrested and taken away. And this in a town where nothing had happened during the Rising.[117] The same thing was repeated in small towns throughout the country. Of the prisoners, 1,400 were released within a week and the remainder were deported to an internment camp at Frongoch in Wales. But the damage had been done.

Taken together with the executions and the rumours emerging of the killing of civilians by British troops in Dublin, the repression of the Rising rapidly alienated nationalist public opinion. In Galway, where crowds had pelted the Volunteers with mud after their arrest, the police reported shortly afterwards that, "the alleged excesses committed by the military in Dublin, and the executions of the leaders of the insurrection subsequently stirred up a considerable amount of sympathy for the rebels, even amongst persons who were hitherto regarded as loyal."[118]

Tim Healy, an Irish Party member, who had been bitterly hostile to the "Sinn Feiners", was even more antagonized by the military occupation of Dublin after the Rising: "among moderate Catholics who are intensely loyal, I find nothing but Sinn Fein sentiment...

The looting of the soldiers, downright robbery and ruffianism against innocent people – the shocking ill-treatment of the prisoners, the insolence of the military in the streets, the foul language used to women and the incompetence shown, all have aroused the contempt and hatred for which there is no parallel in our days."[119]

In Parliament, John Dillon, the deputy leader of the Irish Party, railed against the executions and wholesale arrests: "you are doing everything possible to conceivable to madden the Irish people… you are letting loose a river of blood… it is the first rebellion in Ireland where you ever had the majority on your side, it is the fruit of our life work… and now you are washing out our life work in a sea of blood." Nationalist opinion on the Rising swung rapidly from it being a "mad plot" or "German conspiracy", to being a "fight for Irish freedom". The cause of the Rising was put down to the provocations of the Ulster Unionists and the indefinite delay of Home Rule. The rebels were, after all, "our own flesh and blood."[120]

But was the British repression so savage? By comparison with the Paris Commune of 1870, also an insurrection in a capital during wartime, where the French had summarily executed up to 10,000 rebels and sent thousands more to penal colonies, the reaction to the Easter Rising was rather mild. What was more, in December 1916, Lloyd George, the new British Prime Minister, freed all the remaining 1,800 detainees. The problem was that much of nationalist Ireland did not really accept the legitimacy of British rule in the first place. In the civil war of 1922–23, the Irish public would tolerate the execution of 77 republican rebels and the internment of 12,000 more by a native Irish government, which they subsequently re-elected with a comfortable majority. The British simply did not have enough support in Ireland to be draconian in a thorough manner.

The new generation, the young veterans of the Rising – de Valera, Michael Collins, Richard Mulcahy, Cathal Brugha, Harry Boland – would go on to build a new Sinn Fein party. In early 1917 they won three by-elections. In December 1918, after leading a bitter and successful campaign against the introduction of conscription into Ireland, they won a landslide in the General Election – burying the Irish Party and the Home Rule compromise for good.

Redmond, both the British administration and the Catholic Church agreed, had gone too far for his supporters in his unconditional support for Britain's war effort. The Rising and its aftermath also spawned a new generation of youthful activists. Ernie O'Malley, for example, only 19 in 1916, went on devote his youth to the Republican movement. Thousands more like him filled the ranks of the new Volunteers, the IRA, in the guerrilla warfare of 1919–1921 – an altogether different type of conflict from the set piece battle of 1916. The British would never make up their mind whether to opt for conciliation or repression of the radical nationalist movement, swinging wildly between the two. By 1922, Ireland was partitioned into two states, the southern one of which, the Irish Free State, was substantially independent.

The Free State fell far short of the dreams of many of the 1916 leaders. It would be, despite efforts to promote the use of Irish, almost entirely English-speaking. Partition and membership of the British Commonwealth, and to Connolly the conservative and capitalist character of the Free State, would not have been acceptable to the conspirators of 1916. Nevertheless, the Free State was independent to a far greater degree than was on offer in Home Rule – it went on to become an independent Republic. Whether this could have been achieved without violence, had the Easter Rising never happened and the path of Home Rule been followed we will never know. What is certain is the Rising, the "terrible beauty", the plot of a handful of radicals at the fringe of Irish nationalist society, was a fork in the road of Irish history, after which things would never again be quite the same.

Notes and References

1 Charles Townsend, *Easter 1916: The Irish Rebellion*, p. 393.

2 Peter Hart puts a minimum figure at 3,269, with 4,418 wounded, excluding another 261 casualties from non-political shootings. Hart, *The IRA at War*, p. 30. This seems like a low estimate.

3 Townshend, p. 26.

4 ME Collins, *Ireland 1868–1968*.

5 See Joseph Lee, *The Transformation of Irish Society*; ME Collins, *Ireland 1868–1968*.

6 Townshend, p. 25.

7 Padraig Yeates, *Lockout: Dublin 1913*, p. 87.

8 Hart, *The IRA at War*, p. 91. Hart writes that constitutional nationalism, "accepted the political regime as it was – was willing to achieve its goals through negotiation and legislation – but defined its role as one of permanent opposition until it could change the regime to put itself in power".

9 Townsend, p. 10.

10 Townshend, pp. 26–7.

11 Richard English, *Ernie O'Malley: IRA Intellectual*, p. 107.

12 Padraig Yeates, *Lockout: Dublin 1913*, pp. 259–65.

13 Anne Ryan, *Witnesses: Inside the Easter Rising*, p. 133. Mass Rocks were illicit places of worship when public practice of Catholicism was banned. The Famine was a calamity in 1845–48, when over a million people died in Ireland. Nationalists blamed the British government for allowing the Famine to happen, and the Anglo-Irish social system or 'landlordism' for accentuating it. Oliver Plunkett was a Catholic Bishop martyred in the 17th Century. Wolfe Tone, Henry Joy McCracken and Sheares were Protestant leaders of the United Irishmen, who led a republican insurrection against British rule in 1798. Robert Emmet was a (Protestant) nationalist revolutionary who led another failed rebellion in Dublin in 1803. All the four above were executed by the British.

14 Coogan, *1916: The Easter Rising*, p. 108.

15 Lee, pp. 133–40.

16 Ibid.

17 ME Collins, *Ireland 1868–1968*, pp. 111–12.

18 Townsend, pp. 52–3.

19 Coogan, p. 60.

20 Fitzpatrick in a military history of Ireland, p. 397.

21 www.firstworldwar.com/source/irishproclamation1916.htm

22 Owen McGee, 'Who were the Fenian Dead? The IRB and the Background to the 1916 Rising' in Doherty &

Keogh (eds), *1996: The Long Revolution*, p. 103.

23 Lee, p. 74.

24 Ibid. p. 75.

25 McGee, in *1996: The Long Revolution*, p. 108.

26 Fergus Campbell, *Land and Revolution: Nationalist Politics in the West of Ireland 1891–1921*, p. 190. Pádraig Óg Ó Ruairc, *Blood on the Banner: the Republican Struggle in Clare*, pp. 27–9.

27 Richard English, *Irish Freedom: A History of Nationalism in Ireland*, p. 272.

28 Townshend, p. 68.

29 Townshend, p. 13.

30 Collins, p. 174.

31 Lenihan, *Consolidating Conquest: Ireland 1603–1727*, pp. 238–9.

32 Tom Garvin, *The Evolution of Irish Nationalist Politics*, p. 118.

33 Padraig Yeates, *Lockout: Dublin 1913*, pp. 86–7.

34 Townsend, pp. 11–12.

35 English, *Irish Freedom: A History of Nationalism in Ireland*, p. 264.

36 English, *Irish Freedom: A History of Nationalism in Ireland*, p. 264.

37 Tim Pat Coogan, *1916: The Easter Rising*, p. 26.

38 Hart, *The I.R.A. and its Enemies: Violence and Community in Cork 1916–1923*, p. 47.

39 Desmond Fitzgerald, *Memoirs of Desmond Fitzgerald, 1913–1916*, p. 80.

40 Townshend, pp. 68–70.

41 Ryan, *Witnesses: Inside the Easter Rising*, p. 82.

42 Townsend, p. 192.

43 Townsend, p. 75.

44 Ernie O'Malley, *On Another Man's Wound*, p. 29.

45 Jérôme aan de Wiel, . 'Europe and the Irish Crisis, 1900–1917' in Doherty & Keogh (eds) *1916: The Long Revolution 1916*, pp. 38–9.

46 Leon O Broin, *The Chief Secretary: Augustine Birrell in Ireland*, pp. 160–8.

47 Coogan, p. 74.

48 Jérôme aan de Wiel, pp. 39–40.

49 Townsend, p. 143. British military Intelligence calculated they had 4,800 rifles, shotguns and revolvers in their possession, along with home-made grenades and bayonets.

50 T Ryle Dwyer, *Tans, Terror and Troubles: Kerry's Real Fighting Story*, pp. 84–5. Townsend, pp. 129–30.

51 Townsend, pp. 136–9.

52 Ryan, pp. 86–93; Townsend, pp. 221–4.

53 Hart, *The I.R.A. and its Enemies: Violence and Community in Cork 1916–1923*, pp. 47–9.

54 Campbell, *Land and Revolution: Nationalist Politics in the West of Ireland 1891–1921*, pp. 207–20.

55 Townshend, pp. 240–2.

56 Townsend, p. 123.

57 James Stephens, *The Insurrection in Dublin*, pp. 3–7.

58 O'Malley, *On Another Man's Wound*, pp. 34–5.

59 Ibid.

60 O'Malley *On Another Man's Wound*, pp. 37–8.

61 O'Malley, p. 39.

62 Annie Ryan, *Witnesses: Inside the Easter Rising*, p. 121.

63 Townshend, p. 174.

64 Stephens, p. 18.

65 Townsend.

66 Coogan, p. 107.

67 Ibid.

68 Paul O'Brien, *Blood on the Streets: 1916 & The Battle for Mount Street Bridge*, pp. 22–3.

69 Townshend, p. 163.

70 Ibid. p. 177.

71 Townshend; Coogan.

72 Townshend, pp. 263–4.

73 Townshend, p. 191.

74 Stephens p. 26; Coogan.

75 Stephens.

76 Townshend.

77 Anne Ryan *Witnesses: Inside the Easter Rising*, p. 158.

78 Coogan, pp. 124–5.

79 Coogan, p. 122.

80 O'Brien, *Blood on the Streets: 1916 & The Battle for Mount Street Bridge*, p. 36.

81 Townshend, p. 195.

82 O'Brien, p. 43.

83 Max Caulfield, *The Easter Rebellion*, p. 251.

84 O'Brien, p. 69.

85 O'Brien, p. 83. However not all of the Sherwood Foresters casualties were fatalities. The *Irish Times* published the military's official list of casualties on May 11, which listed 4 officers and 24 other ranks of the Sherwood Foresters killed, along with a much larger number of wounded. Declan Kilberd, *1916, Rebellion Handbook*, pp. 50–5.

86 Caulfield, pp. 287–92.

87 Ryan, *Witnesses: Inside the Easter Rising*, pp. 128–33.

88 Caulfield; Townshend.

89 Coogan, pp. 152–5.

90 Caulfield pp. 338–40.

91 Townshend; Coogan; Caulfield.

92 Townsend.

93 Stephens, p. 67.

94 Townshend, pp. 246–50.

95 Ibid. p. 252.

96 Ryan, p. 135.

97 Townshend, pp. 250–1.

98 Caulfield, p. 355.

99 Ryan, *Witnesses: Inside the Easter Rising*, p. 135.

100 Stephens, p. 39.

101 Ibid. p. 57.

102 Townsend, p. 267.

103 Ruán O'Donnell ed, *The Impact of the 1916 Rising: Among the Nations*, Irish Academic Press Dublin 2008, pp. 196–7.

104 O'Malley, pp. 43–7.

105 Townsend, p. 393.

106 Coogan, pp. 145–6.

107 Ibid. p. 168.

108 Coogan, p. 155.

109 Townshend, pp. 293–4.

110 Caulfield, p. 198.

111 Caulfield, p. 240.

112 Townshend, p. 293.

113 Caulfield, p. 279.

114 Caulfield, p. 305.

115 Wheatley, p. 65.

116 Townsend, p. 274.

117 Michael Wheatley, '"Irreconcilable Enemies" or "Flesh and Blood": the Irish Party and the Easter Rebels', in Doherty & Keogh (eds), *1916: The Long Revolution*, p. 74.

118 Campbell, *Land and Revolution: Nationalist Politics in the West of Ireland 1891–1921*, p. 222.

119 Maurice Walsh, *The News from Ireland: Foreign Correspondents and the Irish Revolution*, p. 54.

120 Townshend, p. 269.

Bibliography

Andrews, Todd. *Dublin Made Me.* Dublin: Lilliput Press, 2002.

Bartlett, Thomas & Jeffrey, Keith. *A Military History of Ireland.* Cambridge: Cambridge University Press, 1997.

Campbell, Fergus. *Land and Revolution: Nationalist Politics in the West of Ireland 1891–1921.* Oxford: Oxford University Press, 2008.

Caulfield, Max. *The Easter Rebellion.* London: Four Square Books, 1963

Coleman, Marie. *County Longford and the Irish Revolution 1910–1923.* Dublin: Irish Academic Press, 2006.

Collins, M.E.. *Ireland 1868–1968.* Dublin: The Educational Company of Ireland, 1993.

Coogan, Tim Pat. *Michael Collins.* London: Arrow Books, 1991.

Coogan, Tim Pat. *1916: The Easter Rising.* London: Phoenix, 2005.

Doherty, Gabriel & Keogh, Dermot (eds). *1916: The Long Revolution.* Cork: Mercier Press, 2007.

Dwyer, T Ryle *Tans, Terror and Troubles: Kerry's Real Fighting Story.* Cork: Mercier Press, 2001.

English, Richard. *Ernie O'Malley: IRA Intellectual.* Oxford: Oxford University Press, 1998.

English, Richard. *Irish Freedom: A History of Nationalism in Ireland*. London: Macmillan, 2006.

Fitzgerald, Desmond. *Memoirs of Desmond Fitzgerald, 1913–1916*. London: Routledge & Kegan Paul, 1968.

Garvin, Tom. *The Evolution of Irish Nationalist Politics*. (1981) Dublin: Gill & Macmillan, 2005.

Hart, Peter. *The I.R.A. and its Enemies: Violence and Community in Cork 1916–1923*. Oxford: Clarendon Press, 1999.

Hart, Peter. *Mick: The Real Michael Collins*. London: Macmillan, 2006.

Hart, Peter. *The I.R.A. at War, 1916–1923*. Oxford: Oxford University Press, 2005.

Kilberd, Declan (ed). *1916, Rebellion Handbook*. Dublin: Mourne River Press, 1998.

Lee, Joseph. *The Modernisation of Irish Society 1848–1918*. (1973). Dublin: Gill & Macmillan, 2008.

Lenihan, Padraig. *Consolidating Conquest: Ireland 1603–1727*. Essex: Pearson, 2008.

McGee, Owen. 'Who were the Fenian Dead? The IRB and the Background to the 1916 Rising' in Doherty & Keogh (eds), *1996: The Long Revolution*.

Nevin Donal (ed). *James Larkin: Lion of the Fold*. Dublin: Gill & Macmillan, 1998.

O'Brien, Paul. *Blood on the Streets: 1916 & The Battle for Mount Street Bridge.* Cork: Mercier Press, 2008.

Ó Broin, Leon. *The Chief Secretary: Augustine Birrell in Ireland.* London: Chatto &Windus, 1969.

O'Donnell, Ruán (ed). *The Impact of the 1916 Rising: Among the Nations.* Dublin: Irish Academic Press, 2008.

O'Malley, Ernie. *On Another Man's Wound.* Dublin: Anvil Books, 2002.

Ó Ruairc, Pádraig Óg. *Blood on the Banner: the Republican Struggle in Clare.* Cork: Mercier Press, 2009.

Ryan, Annie. *Witnesses: Inside the Easter Rising.* Dublin: Liberty Press, 2005.

Stephens, James. *The Insurrection in Dublin.* (1916) Gerrards Cross, Buckinghamshire: Colin Smythe, 1992.

Townshend Charles. *Easter 1916: The Irish Rebellion.* London: Penguin, 2006.

Yeates, Padraig. *Lockout: Dublin 1913.* Dublin: Gill & Macmillan, 2008.

Walsh, Maurice. *The News from Ireland: Foreign Correspondents and the Irish Revolution.* London: I.B.Tauris, 2008.

Wiel, Jérôme aan de. 'Europe and the Irish Crisis, 1900–1917' in Doherty & Keogh (eds) *1916: The Long Revolution.* Cork: Mercier Press, 2007.

Wheatley, Michael. '"Irreconcilable Enemies" or "Flesh and Blood": the Irish Party and the Easter Rebels', in Doherty & Keogh (eds), *1916: The Long Revolution*. Cork: Mercier Press, 2007.

www.ingramcontent.com/pod-product-compliance
Lightning Source LLC
Chambersburg PA
CBHW071635040426
42452CB00009B/1637